What Is Weather?

by Ellen Lawrence

Consultants:

Suzy Gazlay, MA
Recipient, Presidential Award for Excellence in Science Teaching

Kimberly Brenneman, PhD
National Institute for Early Education Research, Rutgers University
New Brunswick, New Jersey

BEARPORT
PUBLISHING

New York, New York

Credits

Cover, © Brandon Alms/Shutterstock; 4–5, © leonid_tit/Shutterstock; 6L, Evgeny Tomeev/Shutterstock; 6R, © Anton Vengo/ Purestock/Superstock; 7, © Jim Brandenburg/Minden Pictures/FLPA; 7TR, © Evgeny Tomeev/Shutterstock; 8, © Andrey Armyagov/ Shutterstock; 9, © Brandon Alms/Shutterstock; 10, © Scott Camazine/Science Photo Library; 11, © Anna Jurkovska/Shutterstock; 12, © kavram/Shutterstock; 13, © Bill Frische/Shutterstock, and © HABRDA/Shutterstock; 14, © Subbotina Anna/Shutterstock; 14R, © Monkey Business Images/Shutterstock; 15, © krechet/Shutterstock; 16, © U.S. Air Force 403rd Wing; 17, © NASA/NOAA; 17BL, © U.S. National Oceanic and Atmospheric Administration; 18, © Melanie Metz/Shutterstock; 19, © Belinda Images/Superstock; 19R, © R. Gino Santa Maria/Shutterstock; 20–21, © National Weather Service, Aberdeen, South Dakota; 21C, © Cosmographics; 21T, © National Weather Service, Aberdeen, South Dakota; 21BL, © Kotenko Oleksandr/Shutterstock; 21BC, © Caleb Foster/Shutterstock; 21BR, © EmiliaU/Shutterstock; 22L, © Evgeny Tomeev/Shutterstock; 22R, © Makc/Shutterstock; 23TL, © Adisa/Shutterstock; 23TC, © Bill Frische/Shutterstock; 23TR, © Kotenko Oleksandr/Shutterstock, and © Evgeny Tomeev/Shutterstock; 23BL, © leonid_tit/Shutterstock; 23BR, © krechet/Shutterstock.

Publisher: Kenn Goin
Creative Director: Spencer Brinker
Design: Alix Wood
Editor: Mark J. Sachner
Photo Researcher: Ruby Tuesday Books Ltd

Library of Congress Cataloging-in-Publication Data

Lawrence, Ellen, 1967–
  What is weather? / by Ellen Lawrence.
     p. cm. — (Weather wise)
  Includes bibliographical references and index.
  ISBN 978-1-61772-405-3 (library binding) — ISBN 1-61772-405-X (library binding)
 1. Weather—Juvenile literature. 2. Weather forecasting—Juvenile literature. I. Title.
  QC981.3.L396 2012
  551.6—dc23
                            2011048748

For more information, write to Bearport Publishing Company, Inc., 45 West 21st Street, Suite 3B, New York, New York 10010. Printed in the United States of America in North Mankato, Minnesota.

10 9 8 7 6 5 4 3 2 1

Contents

Flashes and Bangs!

A giant dark **cloud**, many miles above Earth, fills the sky.

Suddenly, a jagged flash of lightning shoots from the cloud.

Seconds later, a loud clap of thunder fills the air.

The weather report was right.

It said today's weather would bring **thunderstorms**.

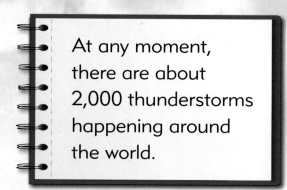

At any moment, there are about 2,000 thunderstorms happening around the world.

A thunderstorm is one type of weather. How many other types of weather can you name?

Weather—What Is It?

Weather is what is going on in the sky and air.

Different places can have different kinds of weather at the same time.

In one place, there may be a thunderstorm, in another place there may be snow.

In yet another place the weather may be sunny and warm.

Temperature—how hot or cold it is—is always a part of weather.

a hot day

thermometer

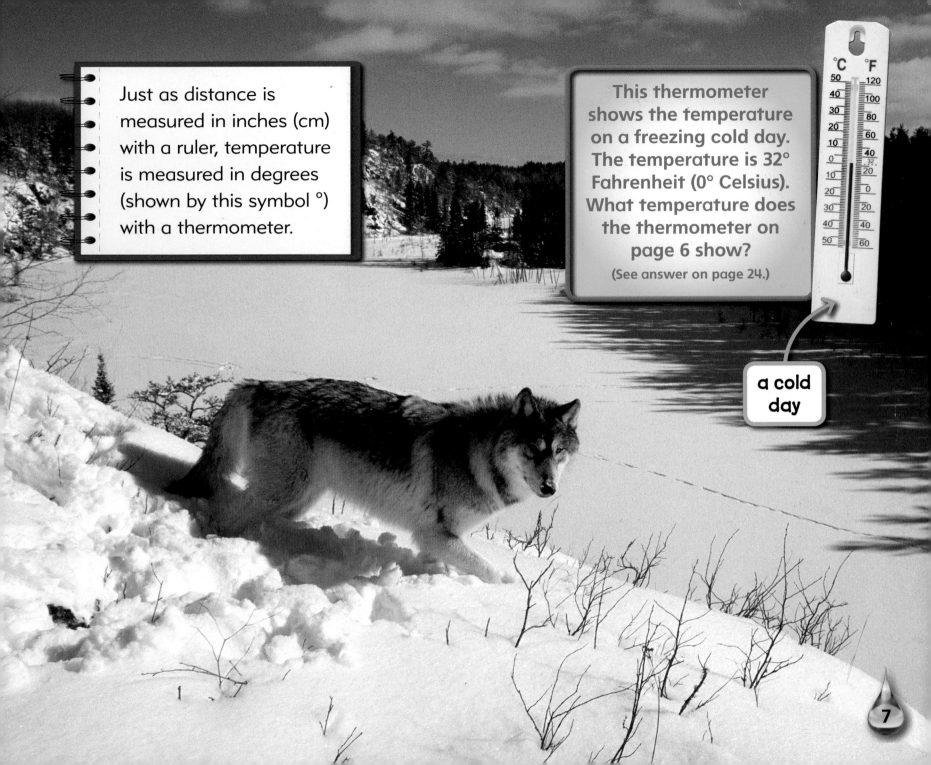

Just as distance is measured in inches (cm) with a ruler, temperature is measured in degrees (shown by this symbol °) with a thermometer.

This thermometer shows the temperature on a freezing cold day. The temperature is 32° Fahrenheit (0° Celsius). What temperature does the thermometer on page 6 show?

(See answer on page 24.)

a cold day

Rainy Weather

When drops of water fall from clouds, the weather is rainy.

Sometimes, lots of rain falls, which is called heavy rain.

Other times, only a little rain falls, which is called light rain.

"Rainy", "light rain", and "heavy rain" all describe the weather.

Sometimes water drops freeze inside a cloud. What kind of weather might that cause?

When tiny, slow-moving raindrops seem to float in the air, the rain is called drizzle.

Snowy Weather

Sometimes the air around a cloud is very cold.

Then, some of the cloud's water drops freeze.

They become tiny pieces of ice that stick together.

Then snow falls from the cloud.

A storm that brings cold, strong winds and lots of snow is called a blizzard.

Snowflakes may look different but they are the same in many ways. How are they the same?

(See answer on page 24.)

snowflakes

Sometimes, snow melts as
it falls from a cloud.
If it hits an area of colder
air as it falls, however,
it freezes again into tiny
bits of ice called sleet.

11

Hailstones

Thunderstorm clouds sometimes produce tiny balls of ice called **hailstones**.

How does this happen?

Wind in these storms tosses water droplets way up high where it is icy cold.

The droplets freeze into little balls of ice and then fall back lower in the cloud.

New water droplets coat the ice balls and they are tossed high again where they refreeze.

This process may happen several times before the hailstones fall to Earth.

thunderstorm cloud

Hailstones are usually the size of a pea. Sometimes, however, they can grow to be the size of a marble, or even a golf ball or baseball!

What type of weather can you hear and feel, but not see?

13

Breezes and Gales

It's not possible to see wind, but it is around on most days.

Wind can be a gentle breeze that moves the leaves on a tree and makes them rustle.

It can also be a gale, a strong wind that can snap branches off of trees!

High in the sky, winds called jet streams move at more than 200 miles per hour (322 kph). Planes flying in the same direction as jet streams use the winds to help push them along faster!

trees blown by the wind

Swirling Hurricanes

Sometimes a huge storm, called a hurricane, begins over the ocean.

It may grow to be 600 miles (966 km) wide—as wide as the state of Montana.

Inside the storm, powerful winds swirl around in a circle.

The winds may reach speeds of 200 miles per hour (322 kph).

If the hurricane moves over land, it can pull up trees and destroy buildings.

Scientists known as "hurricane hunters" fly planes into hurricanes to find out where they are heading. Then they can warn people of danger.

a hurricane hunter inside a plane that's flying into a hurricane

Atlantic Ocean

Florida

eye of hurricane

hurricane

This picture was taken by hurricane hunters inside the middle, or eye, of a hurricane.

What Is a Tornado?

Tornadoes are giant, whirling columns of air with the power to pick up houses!

A tornado starts when air in a thunderstorm cloud begins to spin.

The spinning air moves faster and faster.

Finally, the tornado hits the ground, destroying everything in its path.

a tornado starting

There are about 1,000 tornadoes each year in the United States.

thunderstorm cloud

tornado

damage done
by a tornado

Extreme Weather

Here are some unusual and record-breaking weather events that happened in the United States.

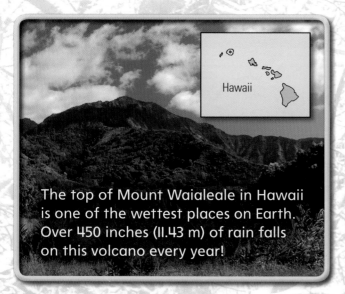

The top of Mount Waialeale in Hawaii is one of the wettest places on Earth. Over 450 inches (11.43 m) of rain falls on this volcano every year!

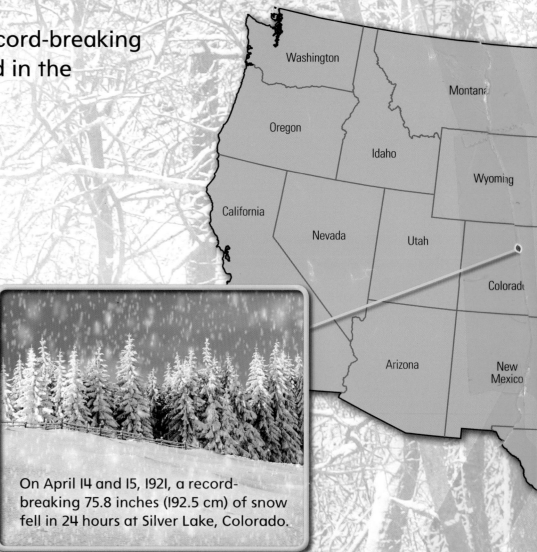

On April 14 and 15, 1921, a record-breaking 75.8 inches (192.5 cm) of snow fell in 24 hours at Silver Lake, Colorado.

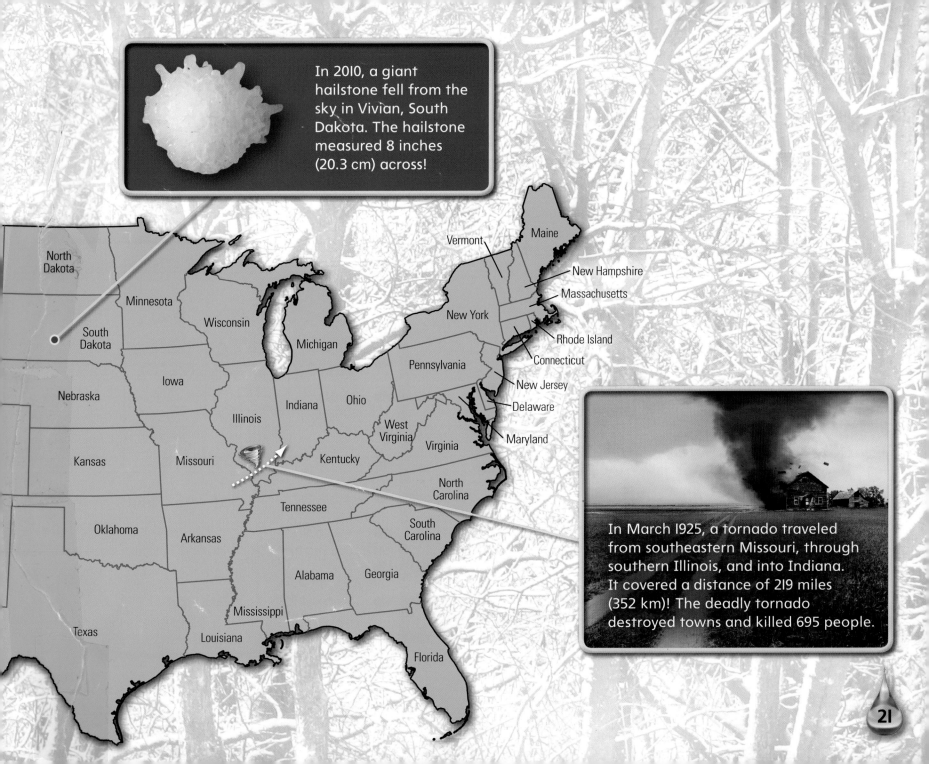

In 2010, a giant hailstone fell from the sky in Vivian, South Dakota. The hailstone measured 8 inches (20.3 cm) across!

North Dakota
Minnesota
South Dakota
Wisconsin
Michigan
Iowa
Nebraska
Illinois
Indiana
Ohio
Pennsylvania
New York
Vermont
Maine
New Hampshire
Massachusetts
Rhode Island
Connecticut
New Jersey
Delaware
Maryland
West Virginia
Virginia
Kentucky
North Carolina
Kansas
Missouri
Tennessee
South Carolina
Oklahoma
Arkansas
Georgia
Alabama
Mississippi
Louisiana
Texas
Florida

In March 1925, a tornado traveled from southeastern Missouri, through southern Illinois, and into Indiana. It covered a distance of 219 miles (352 km)! The deadly tornado destroyed towns and killed 695 people.

Science Lab

Weather scientists, called meteorologists, watch the weather and keep records of what happens. Their job is to tell people what the weather will be like today and in the future.

Be a Meteorologist for a Week

Set up a weather chart, as shown, on a piece of paper.

Then put a thermometer outside.

Check the temperature at the same time each day and record it on your chart.

Add weather symbols, such as the ones below, to show what other kinds of weather happened each day.

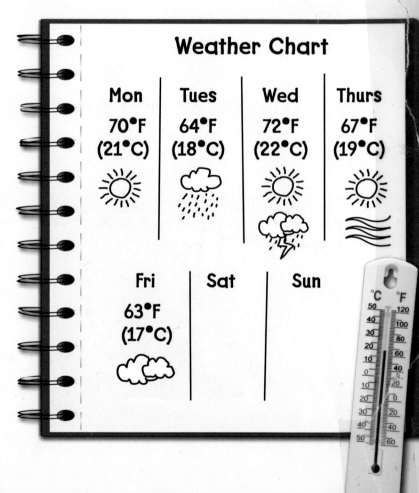

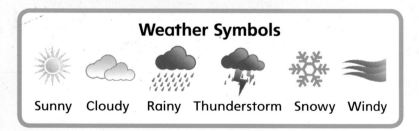

Weather Symbols

Sunny Cloudy Rainy Thunderstorm Snowy Windy

After seven days, describe the week's weather in writing.

Science Words

cloud (KLOUD) a mass of tiny water droplets or bits of ice floating in the sky

hailstones (HAYL-stohnz) small balls of ice formed in storm clouds from frozen water droplets

temperature (TEMP-pur-uh-chur) a measurement of how hot or cold something is

thunderstorms (THUHN-dur-stormz) storms that contain flashes of lightning and rumbles of thunder

Index

Read More

Harris, Caroline. *Weather (Kingfisher Young Knowledge/Science for Kids).* New York: Kingfisher (2009).

MacAulay, Kelley, and Bobbie Kalman. *Changing Weather: Storms (Nature's Changes).* St. Catharines, Ont., and New York: Crabtree (2006).

Mack, Lorrie. *Weather (Eye Wonder).* New York: DK (2004).

Learn More Online

To learn more about the weather, visit
www.bearportpublishing.com/WeatherWise

Answers

Page 7: 100°F (37.7°C)

Page 10: All snowflakes are made of ice crystals and have six points. They form when the air around clouds is very cold.

About the Author

Ellen Lawrence lives in the United Kingdom. Her favorite books to write are those about animals and nature. In fact, the first book Ellen bought for herself, when she was six years old, was the story of a gorilla named Patty Cake that was born in New York's Central Park Zoo.